I Feel Bored

Written by Brian Moses

Illustrated by Mike Gordon

sundance

Kid-to-Kid Books

Red Set	Green Set	Blue Set	Yellow Set
I Feel Angry	I Feel Bored	I Feel Bullied	Excuse Me!
I Feel Happy	I Feel Jealous	I Feel Frightened	I Don't Care!
I Feel Lonely	I Feel Shy	I Feel Sad	I'll Do It!
It's Not Fair	I Feel Worried	Why Wash?	It Wasn't Me!

This edition published
in North America by
Sundance Publishing
P.O. Box 1326
234 Taylor Street
Littleton, MA 01460

First published in 1997 by
Wayland Publishers Limited

Copyright © 1997 Wayland Publishers Limited

ISBN 0-7608-3915-8

Printed in Canada

In the corner today,
we're talking about

feeling bored.

This way to Kids Corner

3

When I feel bored,
I feel like

a goldfish
in a plastic bag,

4

a tiger in a cage,

a hamster
on a wheel,
going
nowhere.

When I feel bored,

I get
in the way.

I annoy my sister.

I tease the cat.

I mess up my room.

When it takes forever
to do the shopping,
because Dad forgot
to make a list,

I feel bored.

When there's nothing to do
on a long car ride,

I feel bored.

13

When Mom has a friend
over for lunch,
and they talk,
        and talk,
        and talk,

I feel bored.

When I'm stuck
in the house
with chicken pox
and everyone else
is out having fun,

I feel bored.

Sometimes, I bore
other people when —

I keep asking
for something
and don't ever stop.

I want
to hear
the same story
over and over.

I watch TV
and ignore everybody.

When I feel bored,

it helps if I
find a game
to play
or a book
to read.

It helps if I ask a friend over
to play.

It helps if I do something helpful, like cleaning my room.

Sometimes, when I feel bored,
I just go outside,
lie down on the ground,
and stare up at the sky.

I look for clouds shaped like
knights, castles, and dragons.
Then I dream
about all the adventures
I could have.

What do you do
when you feel bored?

29

Things to Do in the Kids Corner

On a slip of paper, write something to do. Hide the paper. Then draw a map with an X to mark where you hid the paper. Put the map in a basket. Then, when someone is bored, he or she can grab a map and find "something to do!"

Fold a piece of paper in half. On one half, draw a picture of the most boring thing you did yesterday. On the other half, draw a picture of the most interesting thing you did yesterday.

Singing a song is one way to pass the time when you are bored. Think of a song you like and teach it to a friend. With your friend, make up actions to go with the song.

Brainstorm with a friend some games to play inside on a rainy day. Pick the game you both like the most. Make a poster of you and your friend playing the game.

Make a list of your favorite books. Share the list with friends you think might like to read some of the books on your list.

Other Books to Read

Sick in Bed, by Peter Sloan and Sheryl Sloan (a Sundance *Little Red Reader*, 1995). Being home, sick in bed, can be boring. But the members of this boy's family keep him entertained all day! *8 pages*

Things I Do with My Friends, by Peter Sloan and Sheryl Sloan (a Sundance *Little Red Reader*, 1996). Feeling bored? Here's a book about fun things friends can do together. Other *Little Red Readers* about fun things to do by yourself, with family, or with friends are *Things I Can Do, Family Work and Fun, Things I Do for Fun, At the Park, On Vacation*, and *Children at Play*. *8 pages*

The Cat in the Hat, by Dr. Seuss (Random House, 1987). Two children think that they have nothing to do on a long, cold, wet day. Then they get a surprising visitor, and amazing, unusual things happen! *64 pages*

Bea and Mr. Jones, by Amy Schwartz (Simon and Schuster, 1994). Bea is bored. She's tired of kindergarten, and Mr. Jones is fed up with being stuck at his desk all the time. So, the two decide to switch places. *30 pages*

Danny and the Dinosaur, by Syd Hoff (HarperCollins, 1993). Danny's day at the museum is anything but boring when he makes friends with a brontosaurus! Read how Danny and his new friend spend their eventful day. *64 pages*